SHAPING EARTH

Series Editor: STEVE PARKER

DAVID AND HELEN ORME

QED Publishing

Designer and Picture Researcher: Louise Downey
Project Editor: Michael Downey

First published in the UK in 2010 by
QED Publishing
A Quarto Group company
226 City Road
London EC1V 2TT

www.qed-publishing.co.uk

A catalogue record for this book is available from the British Library.

ISBN 978 1 84835 481 4

Printed in China

Picture Credits

Words in **bold** are explained in the Glossary on page 30.

Contents

What shapes the Earth?

The Earth's surface is always changing. Strong winds, heavy rain, freezing ice, fierce storms and rushing floods alter the land. Our coasts are changed by waves, ocean currents and unstoppable tides.

Ice and water

Freezing and melting ice can crack rocks. Huge **glaciers** of ice carve deep valleys, and rivers move rocks and soil from one place to another.

Volcanoes erupt and build new peaks, such as in the Tengger mountains in Java, Indonesia.

New York City in the United States stands on land that was once thick with forests.

Mighty forces

Many changes that shape the Earth are very slow. But others are sudden and violent, such as powerful earthquakes and erupting volcanoes.

Tell me more!

A big sandstorm can move giant sand dunes many kilometres. Sometimes, sand is blown away from one place, leaving behind bare rocks. This sand may then fill up a valley somewhere else.

Human impact

People are altering the Earth in many ways. We build cities with tall buildings, cut down forests and change the way rivers flow. We drain **wetlands** and push back the sea to make fields for crops. Today, huge areas of land are being shaped by us.

Building up

Huge mountains have risen up in many parts of the world. Most of these mountains formed over millions of years, but some islands have formed in just one day.

Earth's plates

The Earth's hard outer layer of rock, the **crust**, is not one solid shell of rock. It is more like a cracked egg made up of giant, curved **plates** of rock. These jagged plates move slowly over millions of years. When two plates push together, their edges bend and crumple to form tall, sharp-topped mountains.

When two of the Earth's plates move apart, they leave a huge crack in the surface, such as the Great Rift Valley in East Africa.

Exploding volcanoes

In some places the Earth's rocky crust is much thinner. Red-hot liquid rock lies just below this thin crust. Sometimes, this liquid rock builds up so much **pressure** that it pushes through the crust to form a volcano. The runny rock, called lava, may ooze out slowly or burst out as an **eruption**.

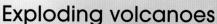

Hot liquid rock from volcanoes cools at the surface and goes hard.

When two of the Earth's surface plates rub against each other, rocks crack and bend up to form mountains, such as the Alps in Europe.

Tell me more!

The remains of sea animals are found high on mountains! Rocks that were once the seabed have been pushed up into mountains, complete with creatures from long ago that are now **fossils**.

7

Wearing down

The Earth's surface is shaped by the forces of wind, rain, frost and ice. These slowly wear away the land. This process is called erosion.

Erosion underground

Rainwater trickles down through cracks in rocks, slowly working its way deeper and deeper. The steady trickle **dissolves** some stones, such as limestone, making small cracks larger. This type of erosion eats away rocks under the surface to form huge caves and caverns – some as large as cities!

The world's largest caves, such as the Mammoth Caves in Kentucky, USA, were made by rainwater erosion.

Tell me more!

In the 1930s, the Great Plains of Canada and the United States suffered severe wind erosion due to drought and bad farming methods. Much of the rich soil blew away in great dust storms.

Power of ice

When water trickles into cracks in rocks and freezes into ice, it spreads out, or expands. This **expansion** forces open the cracks, making them wider. Slowly, over months and years, bits of rock break off and split into smaller pieces. This type of erosion happens underground as well as on the Earth's surface.

This broken rock has been split by water freezing into ice.

Erosion by wind

A gentle breeze can pick up dust and blow it against rocks. Over thousands of years, this dusty breeze can wear away even the hardest rock. Strong winds hurl around larger bits, such as sand and gravel, which can erode rocks into strange shapes.

Wind has sandblasted and eroded these rocks near Colorado Springs in the United States.

Rivers

Rivers flow from high to low ground. On their journey, they erode hills and mountains, sometimes cutting deep **gorges**. Rivers also carry water to dry places, allowing plants to grow.

Rainwater creates mountain streams and waterfalls.

In the mountains

Rivers start out in hills and mountains. Water flows down slopes in small streams, which join together to form larger streams and then rivers. As a river nears the coast, it crosses areas of flatter land and flows more slowly. Sand, mud and other bits settle along its bed and banks. Heavy rain can flood these flat areas, which are known as **flood plains**.

Rivers are powerful enough to cut deep mountain gorges.

Heavy rain can bring masses of water into flood plains.

Out to sea

When the river reaches the sea, it deposits more material. Often, the river spreads out into many channels, forming a **delta**. After this, any material still being carried by the water flows out to sea. Over millions of years, this material builds up on the seabed.

Lack of water

If not enough rain falls, rivers can dry up and even disappear. If people take out too much water, rivers may also shrink and turn into dry, cracked channels.

Tell me more!

Over many millions of years, the Colorado River in the USA has cut a deep channel through the rocks. This created a famous gorge called the Grand Canyon. In parts, it is more than 1800 metres deep!

At 6690 kilometres, the River Nile in Egypt is the world's longest river.

River deltas are made up of many smaller channels.

Ice rivers

North America

Northern Europe

The white areas show how much land and sea were covered by ice 20,000 years ago.

During the last **Ice Age**, much of the Earth was covered by ice sheets and glaciers. Today, glaciers are found only in the coldest regions.

Changing landscape

About 20,000 years ago, during the last Ice Age, parts of North America and Northern Europe were covered with ice. This ice began to melt 10,000 years ago when the world warmed up. Today, although much of the ice has gone, we can still see how it changed the landscape.

Ice is lighter than water, so glaciers and ice sheets float on the sea.

Huge valleys

The biggest changes to the landscape were made by massive 'rivers' of ice called glaciers. These formed high up a mountain where it was too cold for snow to melt. Falling snow piled up higher and higher, pressing on the snow beneath to form hard-packed ice. This ice then moved slowly down the mountain, carving out a huge valley. Today, glaciers are found only in the highest mountains and in the **polar regions**, where it is freezing all year around.

Tell me more!

Under a glacier, melting water can erode rock to form glacier caves. These are exciting and beautiful, but dangerous to explore!

Floating ice is a danger to boats in Glacier Bay, Alaska.

Massive icebergs

Most glaciers melt as they slide down mountains to where it is warmer. Some glaciers, however, are still frozen when they reach the sea. Huge chunks of ice can break off these glaciers and float away as icebergs. The biggest icebergs can be hundreds of kilometres wide!

Glacier power

Glaciers carve out deep valleys and move large amounts of rock and other material from one place to another. These features can be seen where the glaciers have long disappeared.

This U-shaped valley was carved out by a glacier.

Lysefjord in southern Norway is 40 kilometres long. It was formed during the last Ice Age.

Flooded valleys

When a valley that has been made by glaciers runs into the sea, it may be flooded by sea water. This type of flooded river valley is known as a **fjord**. Many fjords are found in some northern European countries, particularly on the coast of Norway. During the last Ice Age, Norway was entirely covered in ice.

Tell me more!

Glacier ice is made from snow that fell over thousands of years. It may contain wind-blown seeds and even tiny animals. Scientists study this ice to find out about the world's climate and life that existed long ago.

Rising land

During the last Ice Age, the huge weight of ice pushed down the land. As the climate became warmer and the ice melted, the ground started to move up again. This movement is still happening today. In Glacier Bay, Alaska, so many large glaciers have melted over thousands of years that the land still rises by eight centimetres a year.

This dry land in Alaska's Glacier Bay was under water 20 years ago.

Coastal areas

Day and night, the Earth's coasts and shores are battered by the sea. Strong sea walls can help to protect some coastal areas from the worst effects of this coastal erosion.

Sea attack

As waves crash into the bottom of a cliff, they smash its hard rock to pieces. Gradually, the waves eat away the cliff base, and the top of the cliff collapses into the sea. Any buildings on the cliff fall into the sea, too.

Harbour walls protect boats from big waves. They also provide people with a solid place from which to fish!

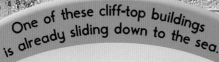
One of these cliff-top buildings is already sliding down to the sea.

New land

Along the coast, waves and currents roll and break big rocks into smaller pieces, such as shingle, sand and mud. These are carried by tides and currents along the coast to make sandy beaches, sand dunes and mud flats. Over a long period of time, these areas build up into new land.

Tell me more!

This land at Eemnes, the Netherlands, was once under the sea! It has been reclaimed by the building of sea walls and by digging channels to drain away water.

These concrete blocks and the reinforced wall protect the coastline.

Tidal times

A tide is the daily rise and fall of water in a sea or in an ocean. As it goes up and down, water wears away seaside sand and rocks, and shapes the shore.

At high tide, waves wear away high parts of the shore, including this harbour wall.

Earth

High tide

Low tide

Moon

Low tide

High tide

The large yellow dots show the bulges in the oceans caused by the Moon's gravity. The red arrows show places with low tides, the green ones show high tides.

High and low
The Moon's **gravity** makes the ocean nearest to it bulge towards it. This is high tide. At the same time, there is another bulge of water on the opposite side of the Earth. Between these two high tides, there is a low tide. As the Earth spins around each day, the bulges move around its surface.

Worn by the tides

As tides rise and fall, they make sea water rush through narrow places, such as between the mainland and nearby islands. The rushing water adds power to the waves and ocean currents. This causes mud, sand and pebbles to scrape along the coast and reshape the shore.

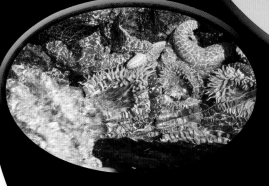

A seashore that is covered and uncovered by the tide is a tough place to live! Plants and animals, such as this sea anemone, have adapted to life both under water and in the air.

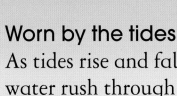

At low tide, the waves have gone and there is no erosion.

When the Earth is between the Moon and the Sun, there are extra-high and extra-low tides,

With the Moon between the Earth and the Sun, there are also spring tides, with great difference

With the Moon, the Sun and the Earth at right angles, there are neap tides with least difference

Shaping the seabed

On land, there are valleys, cliffs, mountains and **plains**. Under the sea, there are similar features, but even bigger! These are shaped by many kinds of underwater forces.

At the edge of the sunlit continental shelf, the seabed goes down into the cold, dark depths.

In the shallows

Around the Earth's continents are shallow parts of the ocean known as continental shelves. The water here is usually less than 150 metres deep and the seabed is mostly flat. Some areas are covered by sand, silt and mud that is carried from the land by rivers. In other places, the tides and currents wash away the sand, leaving bare rocks and stones on the sea floor.

A sonar image of the continental shelf off the coast of California in the United States.

Deep sea

Beyond the continental shelves are steep slopes and cliffs. These lead down to huge, deep-sea plains that are covered with thick mud. In places, there are chains of mountains, narrow gorges and volcanoes similar to those found on land.

Tell me more!

It is difficult to explore the deepest ocean because of the water's great pressing force, known as pressure. Scientists use small robot vehicles called **ROVs** to make maps and take photographs.

Weather and life

The weather is different around the Earth. Hot or cold, dry or wet, it enables plants and animals to live in some places and not in others. Both weather and living things help to shape the Earth.

Lifeless regions
The coldest places on Earth are the polar regions in the far north and south, and the tops of mountains. Here it is too cold for living things to survive, and there are no plants to cover the land. The extreme weather on mountaintops, including rain, wind, snow and ice, wears away the rocks. They break into pieces that roll down the slopes.

Along a tropical shore, mangrove trees protect the land from waves.

Protected by plants

In **tropical** places on Earth, it is almost always warm all year around. If there is plenty of rain too, living things grow quickly. Rainforests cover some parts of the land in the tropics, and mangrove trees grow along the shores. These big, strong plants protect the soil and rocks from extreme weather, such as storms and floods.

Tree roots can force apart rocks and make cliffs collapse.

Severe weather erodes high mountains such as these, making them lower and rounder.

Seasonal changes

Between the tropics and the poles, most places have a warm summer and a cool winter. During summer, the Sun's heat makes cracks in rocks. In the cold winter, the rain and ice make the cracks wider. Over thousands of years, the rocks split apart. Even whole mountains wear down, and the shape of the landscape changes.

Tell me more!

When Mount Pinatubo in the Philippines erupted in 1991, dust darkened the skies for months. This made the weather cool and dull. Many plants, which had protected the land, died.

Animal action

Living things can have a big effect on the land's shape and its features. Even tiny bugs and worms can help to break up rocks and change the flow of rivers.

Roots and leaves

Plant roots stop sand and soil from being blown away. This allows bigger plants to take root and grow in the soil. When fallen leaves gather on the ground, they rot to make the soil richer and deeper.

Tiny workers

The small creatures that eat dead plants and animals, such as worms, slugs and insects, change the land. Their tunnels allow air and water into the soil so that more plants can grow into woods and forests.

Beavers changed the direction of this stream, which is now dry and rocky.

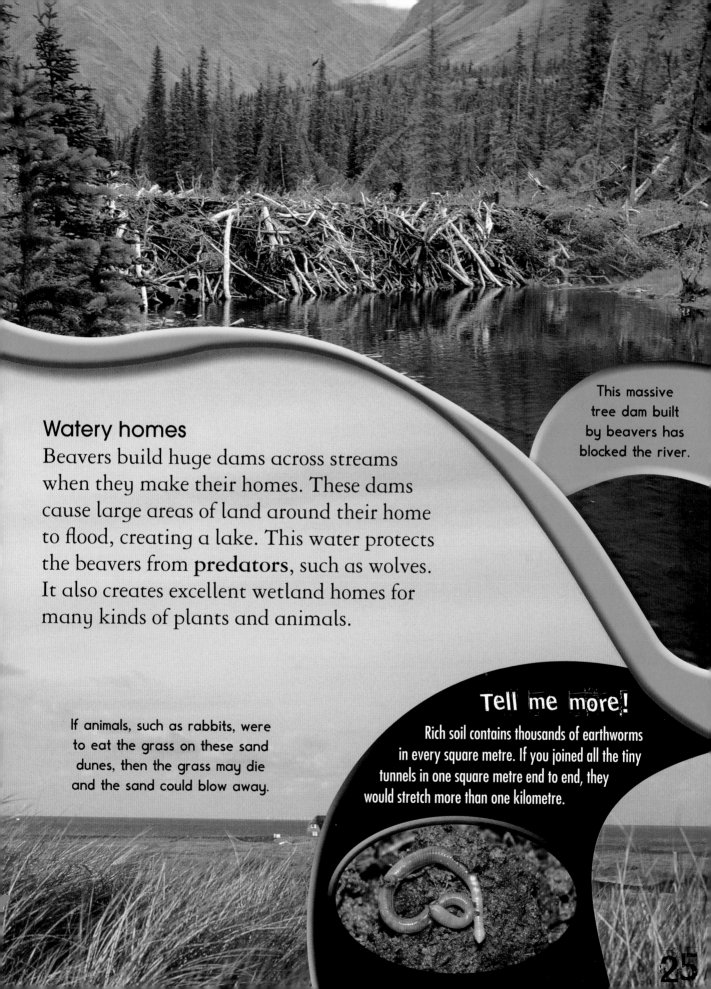

Watery homes

Beavers build huge dams across streams when they make their homes. These dams cause large areas of land around their home to flood, creating a lake. This water protects the beavers from **predators**, such as wolves. It also creates excellent wetland homes for many kinds of plants and animals.

This massive tree dam built by beavers has blocked the river.

If animals, such as rabbits, were to eat the grass on these sand dunes, then the grass may die and the sand could blow away.

Tell me more!

Rich soil contains thousands of earthworms in every square metre. If you joined all the tiny tunnels in one square metre end to end, they would stretch more than one kilometre.

How we change the land

Long ago, people hardly changed the Earth at all. They hunted a few wild animals and gathered wild plants to eat. Today, the landscape is very different. Huge areas are covered with fields for farm animals and crops.

Farming the land

In the past, farms were built where trees and forests once grew. People cut down the trees and used the wood to make their farmhouses, their furniture and other useful things. Then they planted grass on the land for cows, sheep and other animals, and grew crops, such as wheat, barley and rice.

Tell me more!

Bad farming is reshaping huge areas that were once woodlands and grasslands. Every day around the world, an area the size of 10,000 football pitches is turning into dry, desert-like dust.

Losing forests

Changing land from forest to farmland can cause serious problems. This is because fields for crops and animals are not as good at soaking up heavy rain as forests. During a heavy downpour, rainwater washes away the useful soil from fields. This soil then clogs up ditches and rivers.

Flood waters from farm fields can wash into towns and cities.

Worn-out soil

Natural grasslands are much better than farmland at coping with a lack of water. During a long period without rain, called a drought, most farm crops die as they need a lot of water to grow. This leaves the soil without plant roots to hold it together, and it can blow away as dust.

Natural rainforests can soak up very heavy rain without causing floods.

Keeping too many farm animals may make the soil dry and thin.

Some trees lose their leaves in winter, which is good for the soil.

Human impact

When we build houses, shops, roads and parks, wild places have to be cleared. Sometimes, this can have a damaging effect on wildlife and on the natural **environment** in which we live.

Heavy use of water has caused this river in China to dry up.

Roads and buildings

The Earth is being shaped more and more by the people who live on it. New roads and buildings, for example, are using up more and more land. Sometimes, the way a river flows has to be changed to make way for a new town. This can cause the river to flood when there is heavy rain. Also, if people take out too much water from a river, it may dry up completely.

Around the world, there has been a surge in road building.

Tell me more!

One way to deal with the shortage of land for people to live on is to make new land. This has happened in the Netherlands, in northern Europe, where half of the land people live on has been reclaimed from the sea.

Chemical pollution

We change the Earth in ways we can't see. The chemicals we use every day can silently and invisibly pollute the air we breathe, the land in which we grow food and the water we drink. More and more, how we live, and the way in which we make the things to use, is reshaping our world.

Every day, forests are cut down to make room for new towns.

Large cities can cause a lot of pollution in the air and in rivers.

These windmills were built on reclaimed land.

Glossary

Crust Hard, rocky outermost layer of the Earth.

Delta Area of flat land near the coast where a river splits into many channels.

Dissolve Tiny particles spread out in a liquid.

Environment The surroundings, including rocks, soil, plants, animals and the weather.

Eruption When liquid rock from deep in the Earth comes up through the crust.

Expansion Getting bigger when heated or when frozen.

Fjord Deep-sea inlet created by a glacier.

Flood plain Area of land by a river that is regularly flooded.

Fossil Remains of a living thing preserved in rocks.

Glacier Huge river of ice sliding downhill.

Gorge Deep valley cut by a river.

Gravity Force that pulls objects towards each other.

Ice Age Period of time when the Earth was much colder and large areas were covered with ice.

Plain Flat area, usually covered by grass or similar low plants.

Plate Section of the Earth's surface that floats on the liquid, or molten, rock beneath it.

Polar regions Very cold areas around the North and South Poles.

Predator Animal that kills other animals for food.

Pressure Pressing or pushing force.

ROVs Remotely operated underwater vehicles.

Tropical Always-warm places around the middle of the Earth.

Wetland Place with large amounts of water, such as a river, lake, marsh or swamp.

Index

Ideas for parents and teachers

Children enjoy practical activities. Here are some they can do at home or at school.

Making ocean currents
You will need a shallow tray with raised edges, some plain water and a jug of water coloured with food colouring.
• Place the tray so that it slopes slightly. Fill the tray with as much water as it will hold.
• Pour more water gently into the tray at the lower end to create movement.
• Gently pour some of the coloured water into the opposite side of the tray.

What patterns does the coloured water make, and how does it move? The movement in the water creates currents similar to the great currents that move around our oceans.

How water expands
For this experiment you will need a plastic pot, some water, a square of cooking foil that is large enough to cover the top of the pot and be sealed down with an elastic band.
• Fill the pot with water so that there is no gap between the top of the water and the edge of the pot.
• Put the foil tightly over the pot and wrap the elastic band round to keep it in place.
• Place the sealed pot in a freezer overnight.

When you take out the pot, you will see how much the ice has expanded.

Keep a scrapbook of significant events
This is a long-term project for which you should provide a scrapbook and some glue.
• Encourage children to research major events that have affected the Earth.
• These could include recent events such as tsunamis, floods or earthquakes.
• It could also include historic events such as the volcanic eruption that covered Pompeii.
• Prehistoric events, such as the destruction of the dinosaurs, could be additional topics.

My home, then and now
Provide a small kitchen notice board and pins.

• The aim of this project is to produce a wall display showing how your own local area has changed over time.
• Items used can include then and now photographs, historic and contemporary maps, and so on.

Most local libraries have a local history section where children may be able to find old photographs of their area. There are numerous local history websites, which could be a source of similar material.

Glossary games
Provide a dozen small cards, which should be about 6 centimetres by 3 centimetres. Six cards should be in one colour, and six in another colour.
• Select a dozen of the terms defined in this book's glossary on page 30.
• Using a set of cards in one colour, write a glossary term on each card.
• On the cards of the other colour, copy the glossary definitions of the chosen words.

The cards can be used to play various games.
• Match cards with their definitions.
• Select a word card and define the term.
• Pick a definition card and guess the term.
• Spread all the cards on the table so that the writing can't be seen. Turn over two cards. If the word and definition match, remove these cards and carry on. If they don't, turn the cards over again and select two other cards.

Expanding the glossary
Choose other interesting or difficult words from the text and devise glossary definitions for these words. This could be done as an oral or written activity.